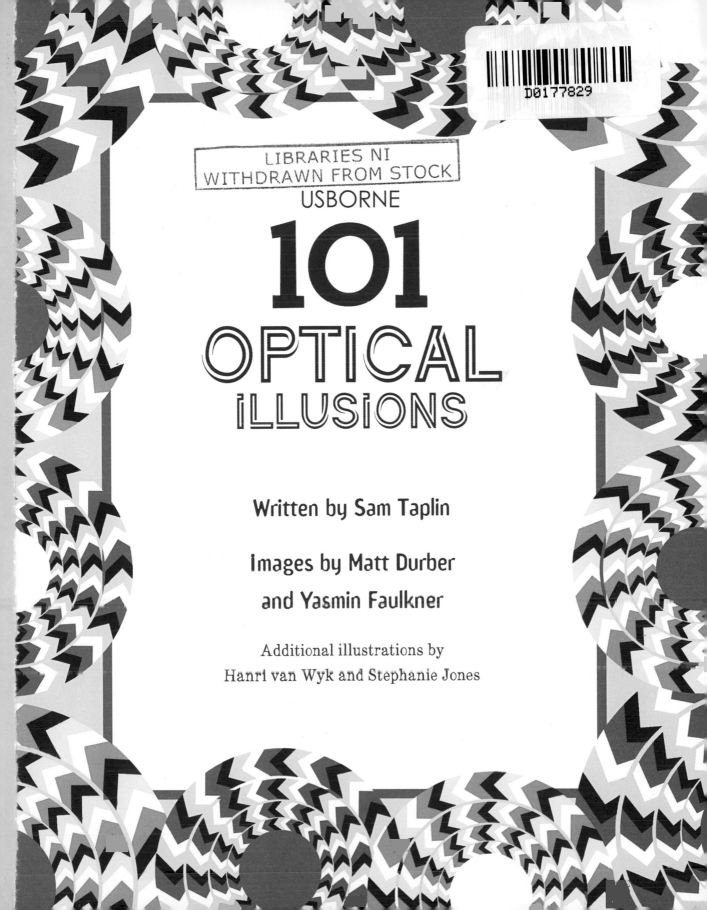

USBORNE

101

OPTICAL
iLLUSiONS

Written by Sam Taplin

Images by Matt Durber
and Yasmin Faulkner

Additional illustrations by
Hanri van Wyk and Stephanie Jones

The magic of illusions

Welcome to the amazing world of optical illusions. An illusion is like a magic trick hidden in a picture – you think you're seeing one thing, then suddenly it's something else. In this book, you'll discover 101 different ways in which a simple image can fool your eyes.

But how do they do it? Here are some of the secrets...

Tilting and bending

One of the simplest and most effective tricks illusions use is to make it look as though straight lines are tilting or bending. All it takes to do this is a series of little diagonal stripes, as you can see here. The two striped lines seem to lean away from each other, but they're completely parallel.

How long?

It's surprising how the simplest illusions can be some of the most baffling. When you look at the two white lines above, it seems obvious that one is longer than the other – but both are the same length. There are many illusions that work like this, playing with the way you see length and size.

Different shades?

Is the blue in the top circle darker than the blue in the bottom one? It seems to be, but both are exactly the same. There are some especially startling illusions that make us see two different shades in this way, when in fact there's only one. Can you see why these two blues look different? It's simply because the top one is "mixed" with black stripes and the bottom one with white stripes.

Impossible shapes

Many illusions create shapes that look normal when you first see them but could never exist in the real world. You can see an example of an impossible shape on the left. Are the prongs at the top of the image, or the bottom? The answer, of course, is both, and as you move your eyes around the picture your mind will switch from one way of seeing it to the other.

Which way?

Some illusions work by removing enough detail to leave your brain unsure what it's actually seeing. For example, look at this cat. Is it facing towards you or away from you? You'll find that you can see it both ways, and it's impossible to say which is the "right" way to see it.

Mysterious movement

Lots of powerful illusions feature images that seem to move all on their own. It's surprisingly easy to make this happen, as you can see above. The red and blue arrows are white at the front and black at the back – and this is all it takes to make it seem as if the red ones are rising slightly and the blue ones falling.

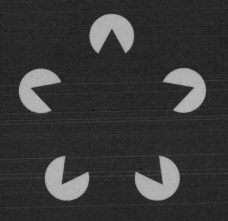

Ghostly shapes

Sometimes an illusion can make you see things that just aren't there. You're probably seeing a star shape on the left, for example, but does that star really exist? It doesn't – it's just the blue shapes that put the idea into your mind.

Special effects

Above is another type of illusion that will leave you seeing imaginary things. The black and white stripes confuse your eyes and make it hard to look at the arrow in the middle without seeing little white flashes racing up and down it. Those flashes aren't on this page – they're only in your head.

You can find many more illusions and learn how they work at the Usborne Quicklinks website. Go to **www.usborne.com/quicklinks** and type the keywords '101 illusions'. But now, turn the page and enjoy the show!

1 Spinning circles

Move your eyes around these pages. Do you notice anything strange?
As you stare, you'll see the circles starting to spin around.
They might even be doing it while you read this sentence.

If you focus on any one circle it will stop rotating completely
– but out of the corner of your eye you'll still see the others
spinning around.

2 Slanting stripes

Are the lines across this image tilted? Or are they all parallel? They definitely seem to tilt, but every line here is completely horizontal. The "tilt" is an illusion created by the pattern of stripes – but even when you know this, it's hard not to see it.

3 Baffling buildings

Look at the top of the two buildings. The top of building A is a fairly square shape, while the top of building B is long and thin. Incredibly, however, A and B are exactly the same shape and size. This seems so impossible that most people have to measure the shapes before they can believe it.

4 Pulsing pattern

Move your eyes around this pattern. Does it seem to pulsate and shift?
If you look for long enough, the middle might seem to vibrate, as
though it's jerking forwards and backwards. Don't stare for too long!

5 Tricky triangles

At first glance, it seems as if the edges of these triangles don't
line up. But in fact all the triangles are perfectly regular. You
can prove this to yourself by checking the image with a ruler.

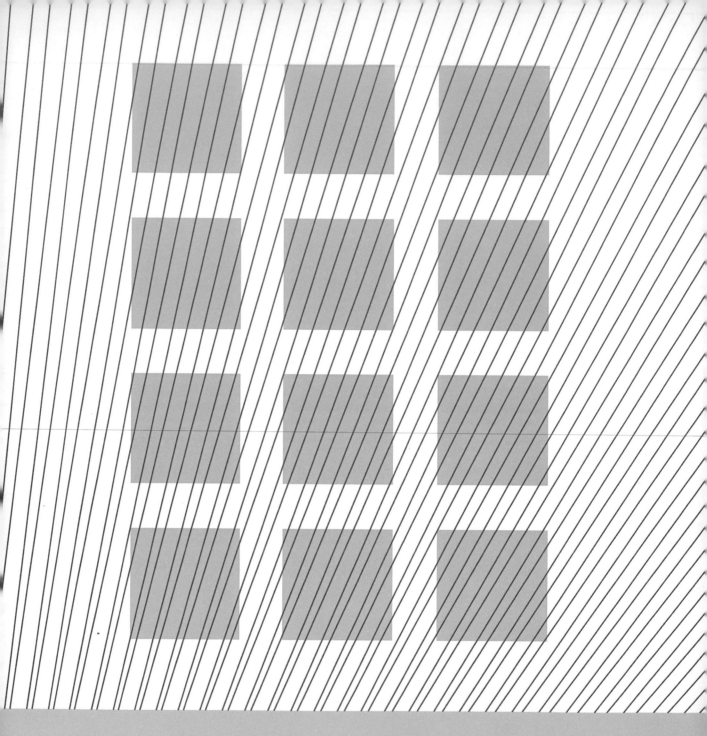

6 Squashed squares

Are these squares slightly wonky, as though they've been squeezed out of shape? It seems so... but every one of them is a perfect square. The diagonal lines are all it takes to create this illusion. If those were removed, the squares would look completely normal.

7 Which way?

Move the book gently up and down as you stare at this image. Can you
see the arrows wobbling? This kind of bizarre movement illusion is created
by the fact that some of the edges of the little squares are black and others
are white. Without that detail, the illusion wouldn't happen at all.

8 Shadowy squares

This image seems to have two types of blue squares in it – dark ones and pale ones. But amazingly all the blue in the middle of the squares is exactly the same shade. It's the pattern of shadow and light around the squares that makes them seem so different.

9 Dark and pale?

This looks very different from the illusion on the opposite page,
but it's based on the same principle. The orange patches on both
giraffes are exactly the same shade, even though the ones on
the right seem a lot paler. Hard to believe, isn't it?

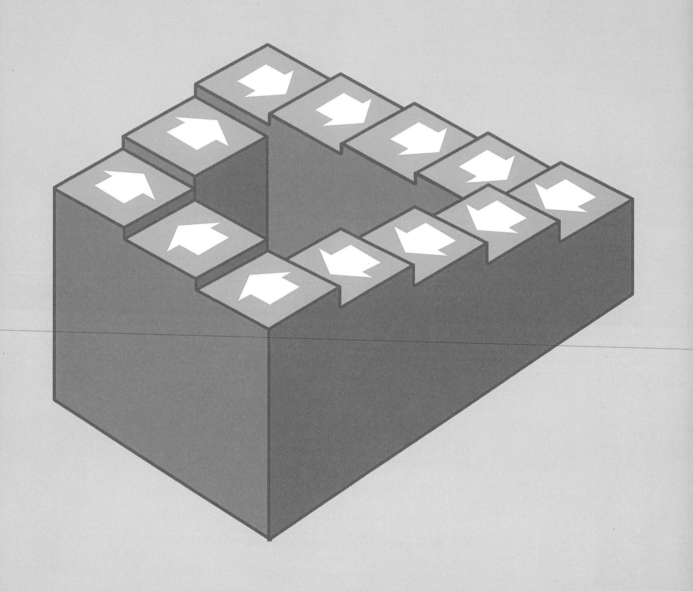

10 Endless staircase

Where is the top of this staircase? And where is the bottom? As you follow it around, you'll see that it actually goes up forever. This famous illusion was created by the mathematician Lionel Penrose.

11 Stars with stripes

Some of these stars appear to have bright yellow stripes and some
appear to have paler yellow stripes. But all the yellow in this image
is the same shade – it's combining it with red or blue that changes
the way you see it.

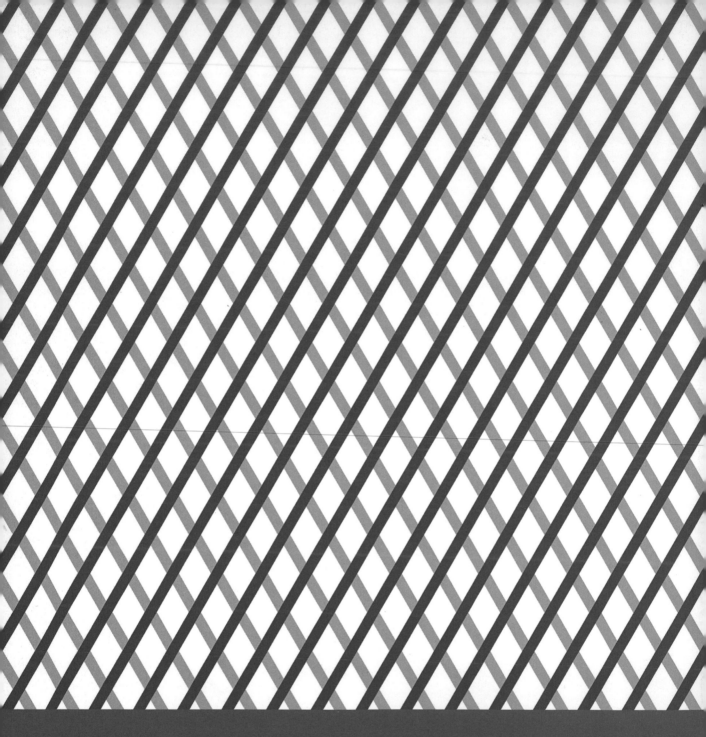

12 Ghostly lines

This image just shows a grid of orange and red lines – nothing else has
been added to it at all. And yet it somehow creates a very odd effect.
If you look around the page you'll see horizontal white lines flickering
across the grid. These lines don't exist, but you'll see them all the same.

13 Distorted shapes

Are the three green circles slightly squashed? How about the red squares? All the shapes are perfectly regular, but the pattern of lines behind them confuses our eyes and may make them appear distorted.

14 Confusing cubes

Could you really arrange cubes like this? At first glance you might think so, but in fact it would be totally impossible. If you start at one corner and follow them around, you'll gradually see why. The more you look at this, the weirder it will get.

15 Strange spiral

Can you follow this red spiral around and around towards the middle?
If you think you can, your eyes are fooling you – there's no red spiral
here at all. It's just lots of separate circles. The spiral effect is created
by the extra black lines among the red ones.

16 Floating umbrellas

The umbrellas on the left-hand page are resting on the ground, while the ones on the right are slightly higher, because they're floating in the air. Right?

Wrong! Look again at each page – both sets of umbrellas are in the same positions. All that's different is the position of the shadows, but that's enough to create the illusion that the ones on this page are higher.

17 Squeezed circles

All these circles look slightly bent, as though they've been squeezed out of shape. But they're all perfect circles. The pattern of black and white stripes confuses our eyes and creates this surprising illusion.

18 Bending edges

Do the red and green squares in this pattern have curved edges? It looks
as though they do... but they don't! All the squares are regular, and it's
the blue squares around them that create the illusion of curved lines.

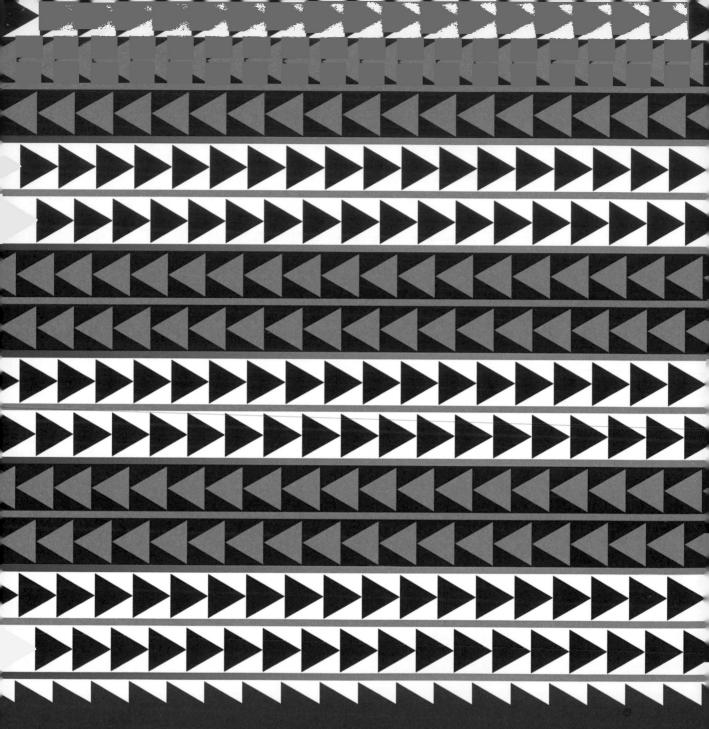

19 Leaning lines

Does each row of blue triangles get wider as it goes to the left? And is each row of black ones wider at the right? It certainly seems so – but in fact all the lines going across this image are parallel and nothing is tilting at all.

20 Middle mystery

Look at the middle section of each circle. Two of them look pale and two seem darker. But actually they are all the same. You can prove this by covering up the rest of each image and looking only at the middle.

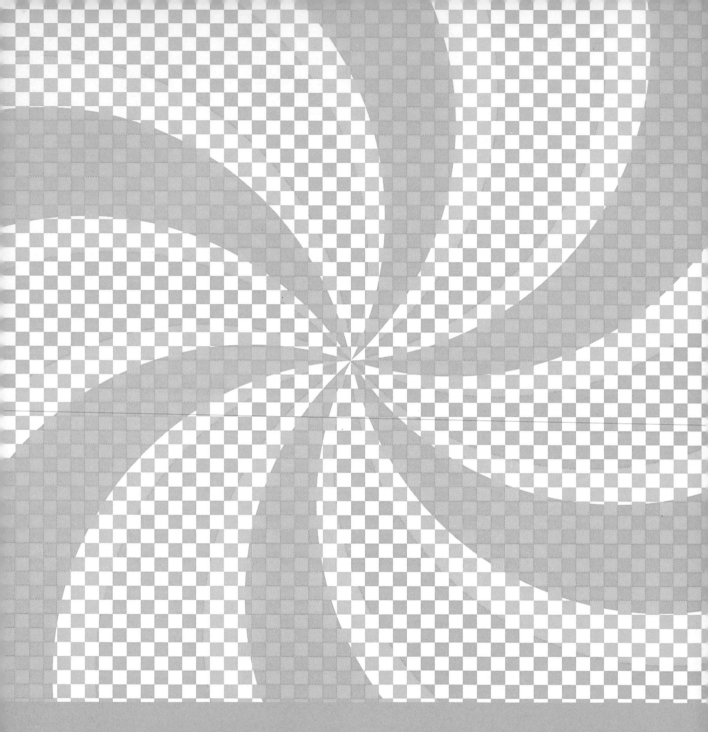

21 Perplexing pink

Are there two different pinks in this picture? Half the swirls seem to have dark pink squares and half brighter pink ones. But all the pink squares are the same – it's the green or white squares around them that change how we see them.

22 How many?

Believe it or not, this whole image is made from just one shade of
green, one shade of red and one shade of blue (plus black and white).
By combining these in different ways, you can create the illusion that
there are many more.

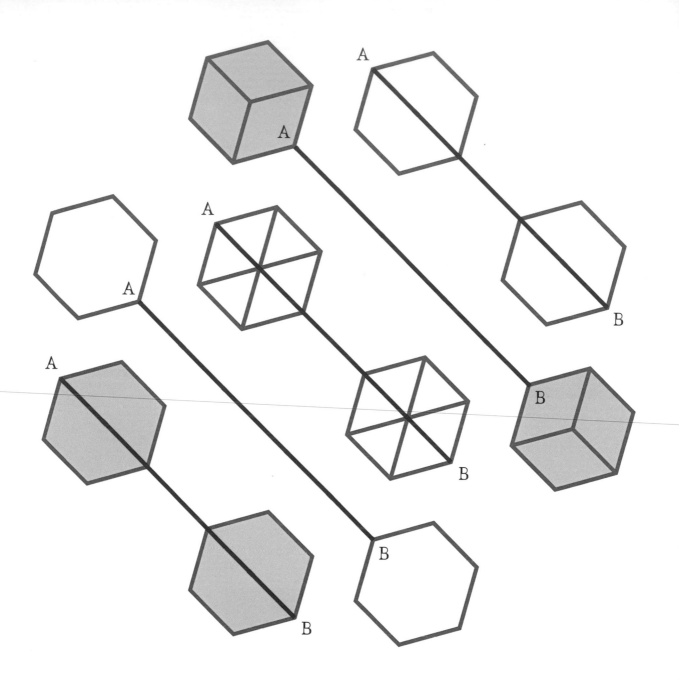

23 Long and short lines

Look at the five red lines on this page, from point A to point B. Two of those lines seem long and three seem shorter. But all five lines are exactly the same length. If you find this hard to believe, measure the lines.

24 Ghostly grid

Look at the gaps between the lines. Can you see little white squares in
the gaps? Those squares don't exist, but it's very hard not to see them.
You might even see the squares linking up to make a grid pattern.
None of this is actually there, but the illusion is very effective.

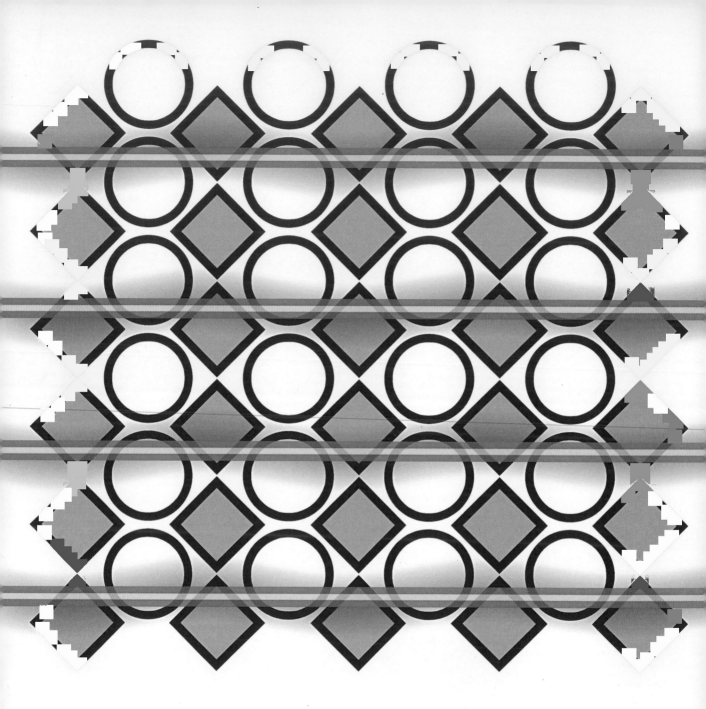

25 Wobbly lines

Look at the four "ribbons" across this page. Do they look slightly wobbly, as though they need to be straightened out? The shapes beneath the ribbons certainly make us see it that way – but in fact the lines are completely straight and parallel.

26 Beach hut baffler

Look at the two beach huts with red and white stripes. Is the one at the top bigger than the one at the bottom? It seems to be... but they're exactly the same size. This illusion works because the hut at the top is further away, which makes us think it must be bigger than the other one.

27 Dancing dots

As you move your eyes around this image you'll see dark dots appearing and disappearing on the white ones. Although the dots definitely aren't there, it's a very strong illusion. If you stare at a dark dot it will vanish, but you'll still glimpse the others all around it.

28 Tilted shapes

Look at the shape at the bottom – are the green lines tilting slightly to
the right? In fact they're not tilting at all, and they line up perfectly
with the green lines in the top shape. You can check this with a ruler,
but the background pattern will still make you see the tilt.

29 Same circles?

At the bottom you can see a dark circle, and at the top a pale one.
But all four circles are the same – all that's different is the
background. This works even when the circles are right next to each
other, as you can see if you look at the two in the middle.

30 Double trouble

This cunning image combines two separate illusions. Some of the vertical stripes look dark and some a little lighter, but they're all the same shade. And the stripes appear to bend and tilt, but they're all perfectly parallel and straight. Nothing is as it seems!

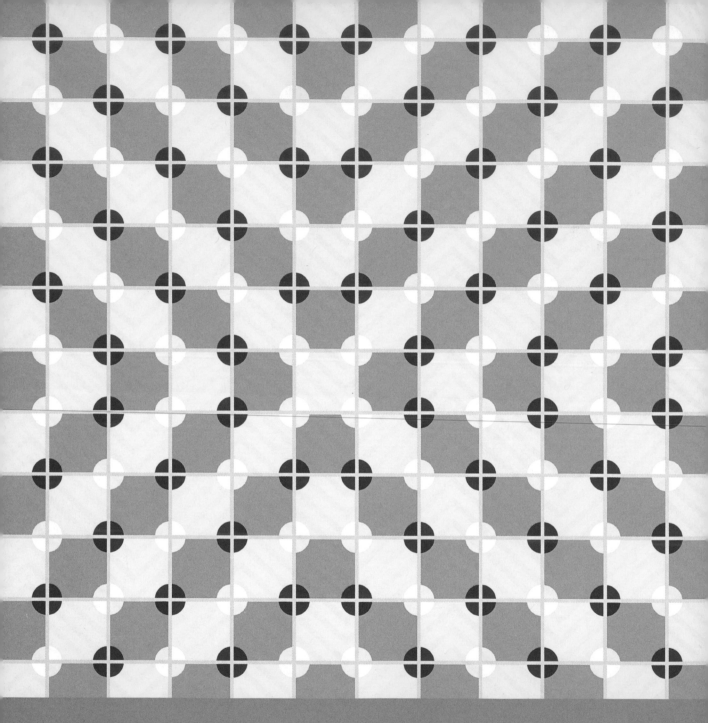

31 Bulging grid

Is the grid of lines bending away from the middle of the page, as though something is pushing it out at you? It certainly seems to be. But in fact the grid is entirely straight. The pattern of circles is what creates this powerful illusion.

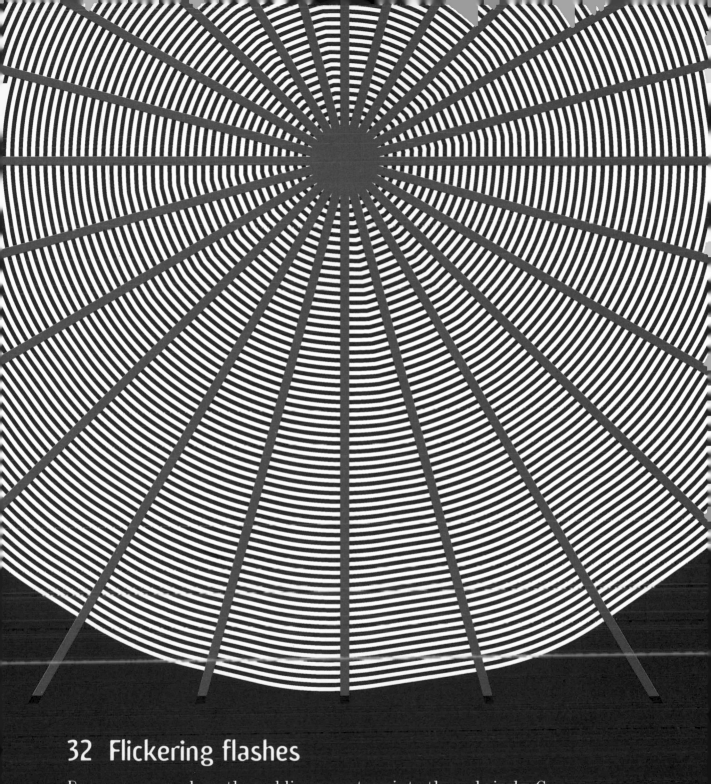

32 Flickering flashes

Run your eyes along the red lines, or stare into the red circle. Can you
see tiny white flashes flickering up and down? These flashes don't exist,
but it's impossible not to see them. It's the pattern of black and white
stripes that bewilders your eyes and makes you see what's not there.

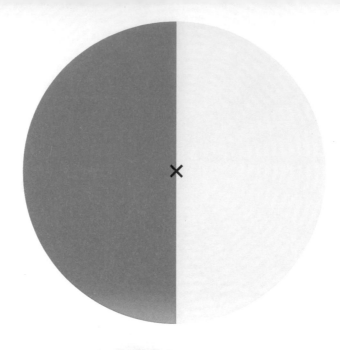

33 Vanishing circle

Stare at the black X at the top for at least 30 seconds, then look at the black X at the bottom. Can you see what happens? The faint blue and yellow circle at the bottom will completely vanish so you just see an orange shape on a plain white background.

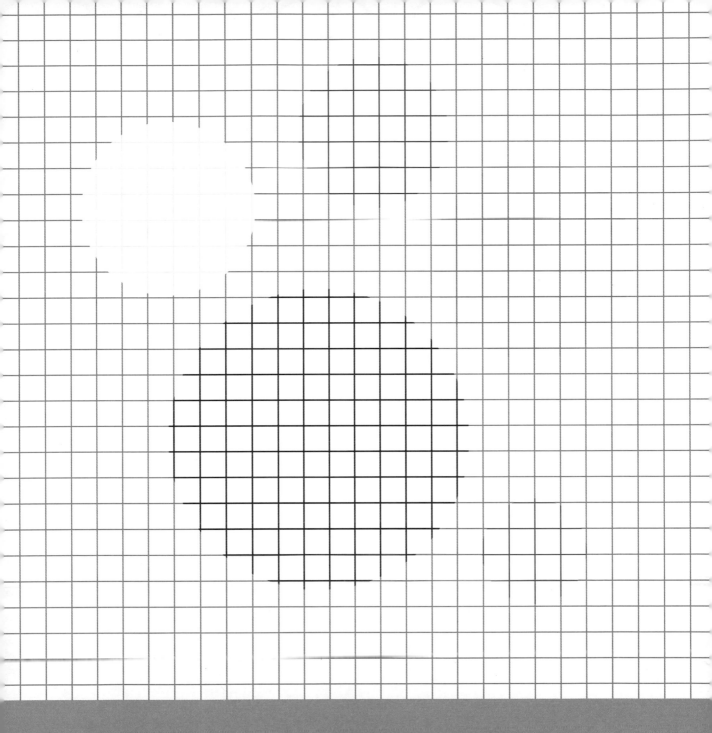

34 Imaginary circles

When you look at this page you'll see circles. Those circles don't actually exist, though – there are no curved lines at all. The shade of each one seems to fill the whole circle, even though the gaps between the lines are all plain white. Can you see all five circles?

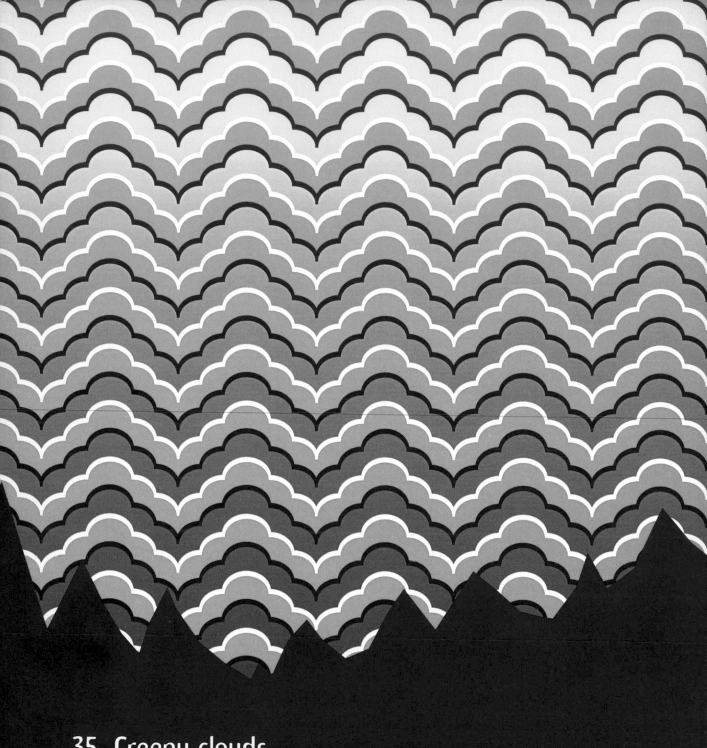

35 Creepy clouds

Stare at the clouds, and move the page slowly up and down. Can you
see how they seem to squeeze together and then apart again? Even
when you're not moving the page the clouds might appear to shift –
if you stare at them you might see them moving slowly down.

36 Bewildering blocks

Take a look at the blocks. Are the yellow surfaces the tops or
the bottoms? The answer is both – it depends how you look at
it. The more you stare, the more you'll be able to make yourself
see it first one way and then the other.

37 Circle sizes

Look at the two yellow circles. Is the one at the front smaller than the one in the distance? You'd think so, wouldn't you, but the two circles are exactly the same size. Although it looks completely different, this illusion works in a similar way to number 26.

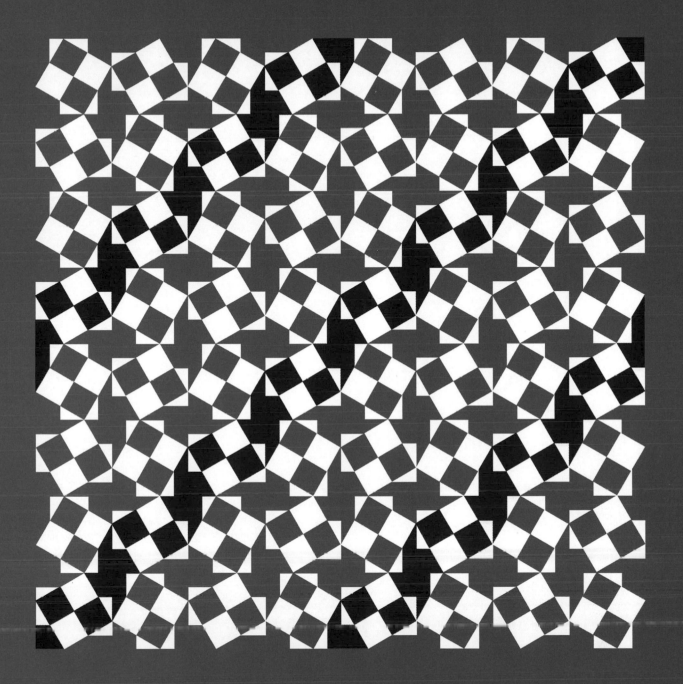

38 How many curves?

Take a quick glance at this image. How many curved lines does it
have in it? The answer is... none at all. It's a pattern made entirely
out of squares and straight lines, but the way they're arranged
creates the illusion of curves snaking across the page.

39 Slanting squares

Do these squares look as though they're slanting in different directions? All of the squares are completely regular and all the edges are parallel, but it's very hard to see this because the little diagonal lines create a strong illusion of tilting.

40 Long and short?

Look at the white line near the top of the page, and then the other white line further down. Is the top line longer than the bottom one? The other lines make it seem that way, but in fact the two white lines are exactly the same length.

41 Puzzling paint

Is the blue paint in the foreground brighter than
the blue in the background? It seems to be, but all the blue
is exactly the same shade. Combining the blue with white squares
or with black squares is what makes us see it differently.

42 Wonky wall

Every row of blocks in this wall is completely horizontal.
But it's almost impossible to look at this image without seeing
them tilting up to the right. Take a look at illusions 2 and 19 for
different versions of this very convincing effect.

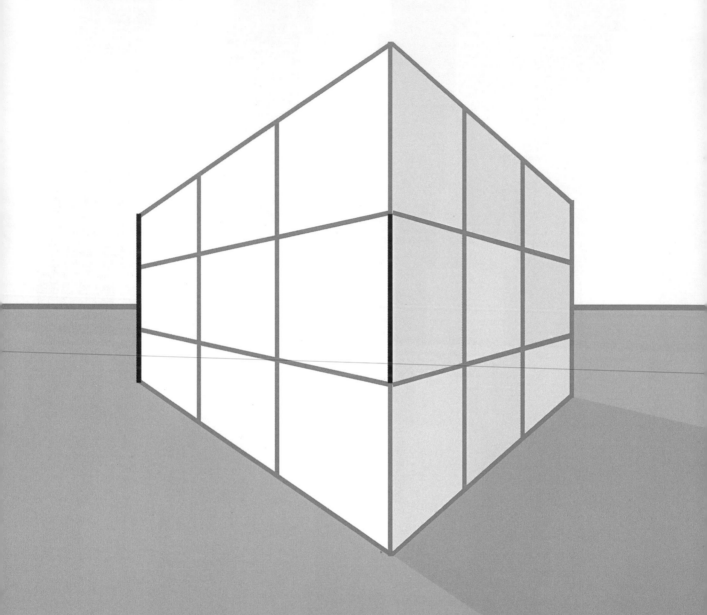

43 Which line is longer?

Is the black line on the left longer than the one on the right? It seems to be, but both lines are the same length. This illusion works because we know that, in the world of the picture, the left-hand line is "really" longer. It's surprising how this fools our brains into seeing it that way.

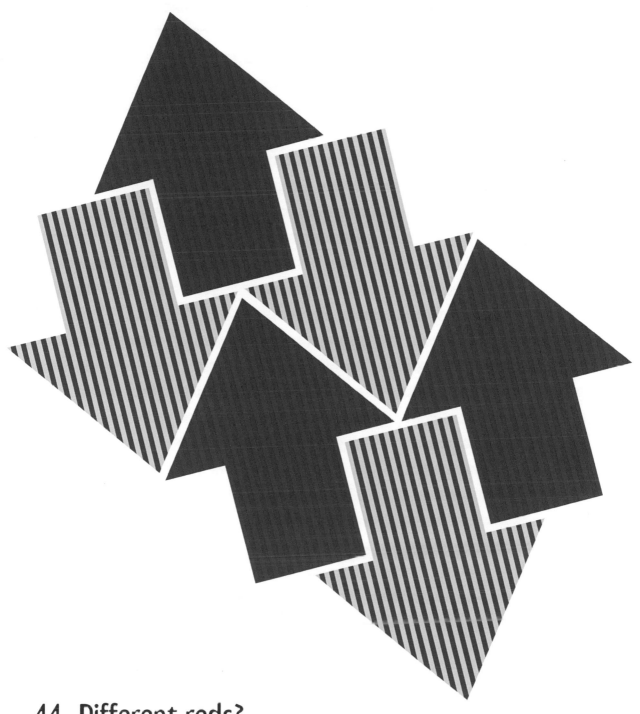

44 Different reds?

The red stripes in the arrows pointing up the page look quite dark, and the red stripes in the arrows pointing down look a little lighter. But all the red in this image is exactly the same shade – it's the purple and yellow stripes that change the way you see it.

45 How many blues?

The foreground of this picture looks dark blue, and the background
seems to be paler blue. But are those two blues really different?
They're not – all the blue in this image is exactly the same. Combining
it with black or white stripes creates the illusion of different shades.

46 Whirling shapes

Stare at this page and move the book around. Do you see strange
ghostly shapes flickering around the middle of the image? No one
is quite sure exactly what causes this bizarre illusion to happen.

47 Strange swirls

There are two separate illusions hiding in this image. The first one is that the black lines going up the page are not tilting at all – they're completely parallel, even though they seem to lean quite a bit.

The second strange thing about this image is a movement illusion.
If you stare at the columns for long enough and move your eyes around,
some columns will seem to rise up the page and others to fall.

48 Puzzling planes

The two small planes on the left look pale blue, and the ones on the right look a little darker. But all of the blue in this image is exactly the same shade. To see how this works, look at the big plane at the top – as you go from left to right, you can see the shade getting darker.

49 Sneaky squares

At first, this just looks like a simple pattern of squares. But look closely at it, and move your eyes from one section to another, and you'll see something very odd. The squares seem to shift and flow in a peculiar way. The more you stare, the more it will happen.

50 Now you see it, now you don't

Stare at the owl's black beak in the middle of this page for at least 30 seconds and try not to blink. After a while, the orange glow around the beak should start to fade. If you look for long enough, the whole picture might start to vanish. Then blink, and it will reappear.

51 Swirling circles

Stare into the middle of these circles and you'll see a weird
illusion of movement. They seem to flicker back and forth quite
quickly before your eyes. If you keep staring, the whole shape
might start to shudder slightly.

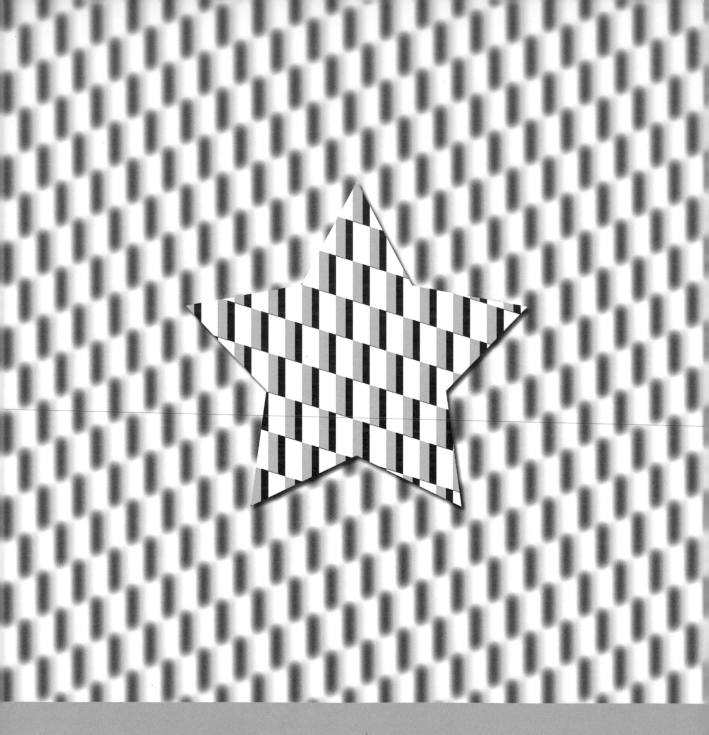

52 Shaking star

Shake the book from side to side, and look at the star in the middle.
Can you see it wobbling slightly, separately from the background? This
happens because of the way the background is blurred – it makes the star
look as though it's hovering above the page, which confuses your eyes.

53 Where's the middle?

One of the three dots on each triangle is exactly halfway up the triangle.
But which one? Surprisingly, it's the orange dot on all three triangles.
If you find this hard to believe you can prove it by measuring.

54 Cake confusion

How can you put all the cakes onto the stand without folding or cutting the page? It sounds impossible but the answer is very simple – look at the separate images and relax your eyes, then let the images drift towards each other until the cakes are sitting in the right place.

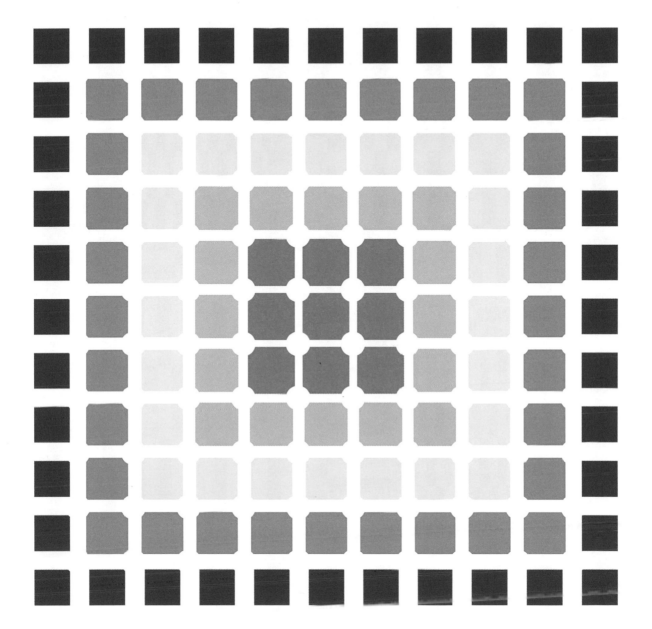

55 Ghostly dots

As you move your eyes around this image, you'll see faint little dots appearing and disappearing at the corners of the squares. The dots aren't really there, and if you try to look at one it will vanish, but you'll still see the others out of the corner of your eye.

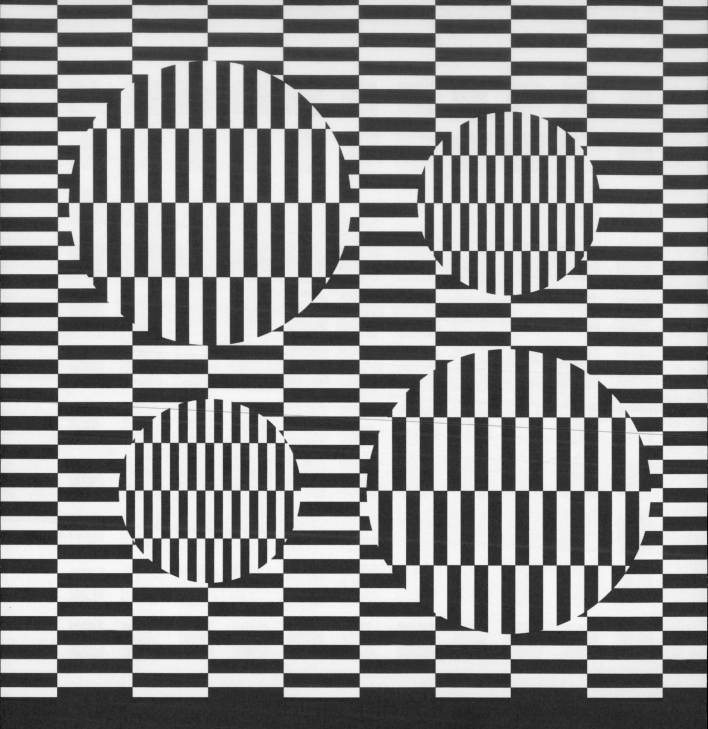

56 Quirky circles

Shake the book gently up and down – can you see the circles wobble? All it takes to produce this illusion is to "cut out" the circles and rotate them against the background. Without that pattern, the illusion would disappear.

57 How many monsters?

Take one quick look at this page, then look away. Are there more red monsters or blue ones? In fact there are exactly the same number of both, but when you first glance there seem to be more red ones. This is because the red ones stand out more, and also because of the way they're arranged.

58 Longer and longer

These three lines seem to be different lengths, each one slightly longer than the last. But look carefully and you'll see that all the black lines are exactly the same length. Simply adding the little red arrows to the end of the lines creates the illusion.

59 Concealed cubes

This image seems like a simple pattern – unless you know the right way to look at it. Tilt the book away from you and lift it up close to your face, then close one eye. If you look again at the picture, you'll see a stack of cubes.

60 Spinning around

Stare into the middle of these circles. Can you see them spinning?
This powerful movement illusion happens because the arrows are
black at the back and white at the front. Without this seemingly
unimportant detail, the circles wouldn't spin at all.

61 Virtual shapes

Can you see anything strange about the white shapes on this page?
The answer is that they don't exist! They're just suggested by the
smaller shapes around them. And yet you can "see" their edges
and they seem to be a brighter white than the background.

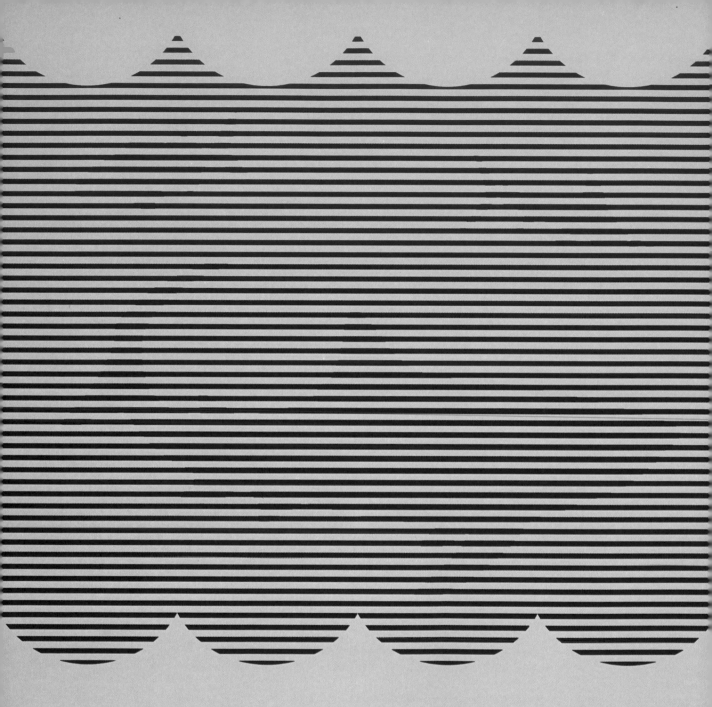

62 Mysterious waters

When you first look at these pages there seems to be nothing on them but a simple pattern. But there's a surprise hiding among the stripes. Try to find out what it is, then read the opposite page.

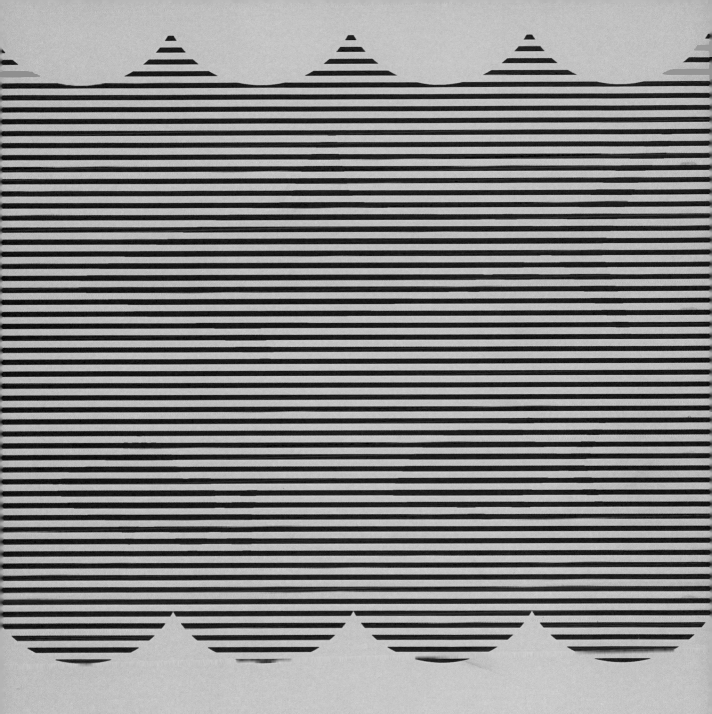

To reveal the secret of this illusion, move it quickly up and down while you stare at it, or look at it from far away. When you do this, you'll see that there's a group of sea creatures lurking in the water!

63 Impossible triangle

This is one of the most famous examples of an impossible shape
– something that looks normal at first but would actually be
impossible to build. Take a good look at the triangle – can you
see why it could never really exist?

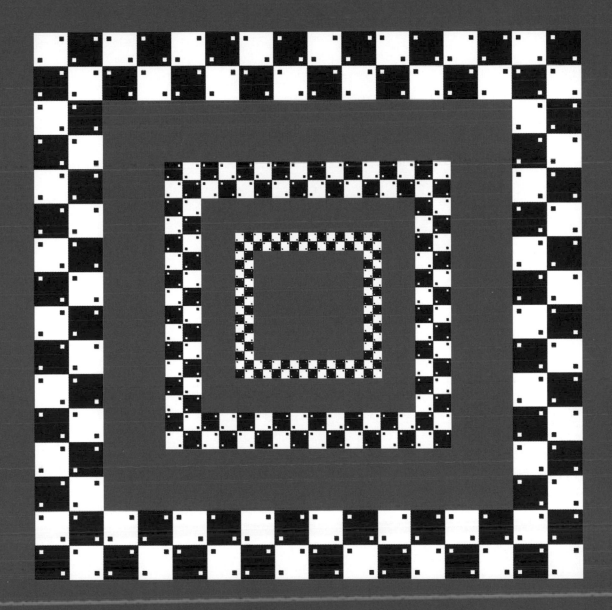

64 Wobbly squares

Look at the two small squares. Do they have wobbly edges?
All three squares are completely regular and their edges are
straight, but the black and white dots create a very convincing
illusion that the lines are wobbly.

65 Which way?

Is this player about to kick the ball towards you, or away from you? It's actually possible to see the image both ways, depending on how you look at it. You'll find that your mind keeps flipping between the two different views of the image.

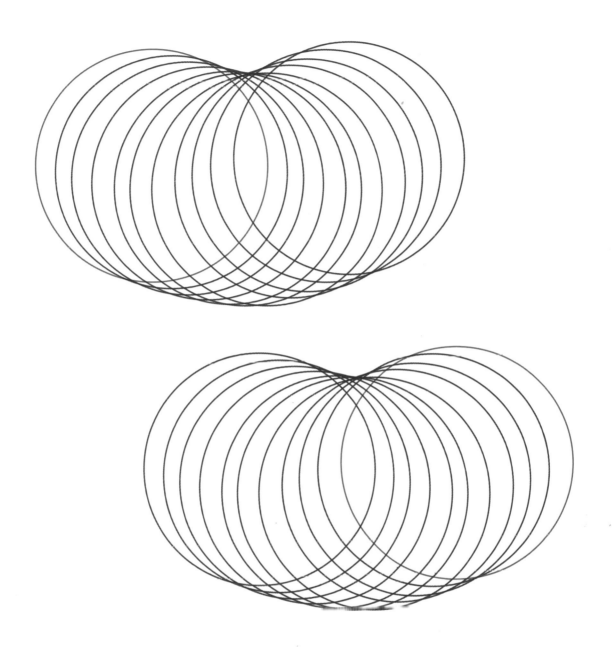

66 Which end?

This illusion looks completely different from the one on the opposite page, but it's actually very similar. Think of these two images as tubes, and try to decide if the orange circle is the end that's closest to you or furthest away. Once again, it's possible to see it both ways.

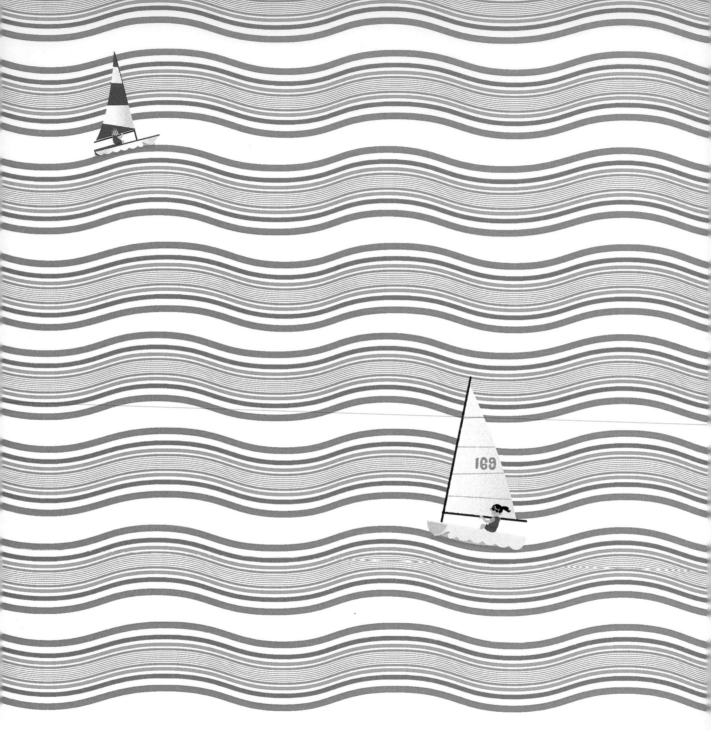

67 Bumpy waves

This image demonstrates how easy it is to create the illusion of something three-dimensional. All you're looking at is lots of wavy lines, but can you see how the waves seem to actually rise up from the page, as though there are bumps in it?

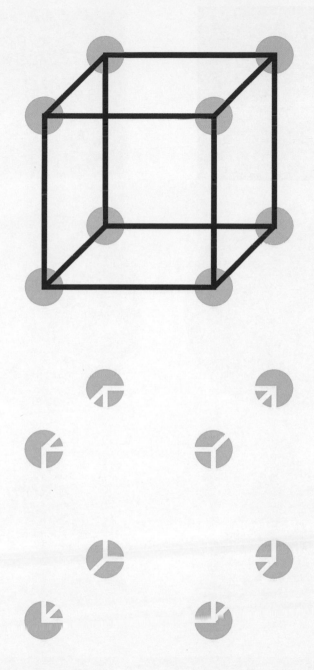

68 Creating a cube

At the top you can see an actual drawing of a cube. Below it you can see
the same type of cube – except that this one only exists in your mind.
There's nothing there except the little circles with lines cut out of them,
but you can still "see" the entire cube, as though all the edges were there.

69 Fuzzy shapes

Look at each pair of shapes. The ones on the right look slightly paler than the ones on the left, but each pair is exactly the same shade. All that's different is that the ones on the right have fuzzy edges – yet this is enough to persuade your eyes that they're not as dark as the others.

70 Twisted shapes

These shapes seem to be full of curves, as though they've been squashed or melted. But in fact there are no curves: the top one is made out of perfect triangles and the bottom one is all perfect squares. Simply rotating the shape and repeating it creates the weird effect of curves.

71 Train trouble

Can you see what's impossible about this picture? Try starting
at the bottom and following each column up to the top. When
you get about halfway up you'll feel your mind "flip" between
seeing it as a column and seeing it as a gap between columns.

72 Same stars?

Look at the middle of the top star – is it brighter than the middle of the bottom one? All the green in the image is exactly the same shade, but the two stars look different because of the different backgrounds.

73 Tilting lines

Each green line seems to tilt slightly upwards as it goes to the right, and each red line seems to do the opposite. All the lines are completely parallel, and all that's needed to create the illusion is the little white stripes.

74 Circle squares

This image shows a series of squares made out of little circles. All the squares are completely regular, and the edges don't lean at all. But because of the pattern on the circles it's hard to see it that way – as you stare into the middle you'll see the squares appearing to distort.

75 Bowed square

Do the sides of the yellow square bulge outwards? The square is actually completely regular, with straight sides, but the pattern of circles makes the edges appear to curve.

76 Devious diagonals

How many of these lines go all the way across the page? Can you follow one all the way across? If you think you can, your eyes are deceiving you! None of the lines goes all the way across, but the way that they fade towards the middle makes it hard to see this.

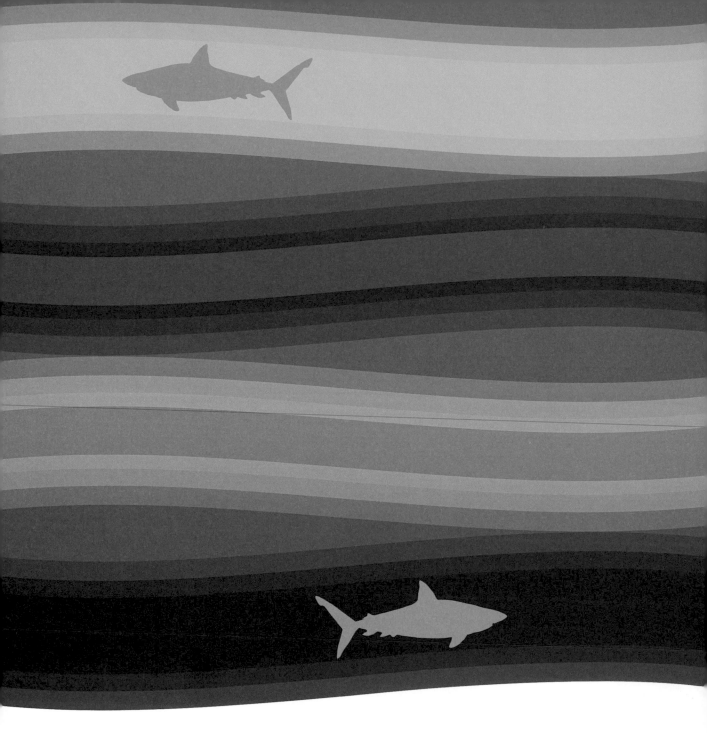

77 Shark shades

The shark at the top looks dark blue and the one at the bottom looks brighter blue. But both are exactly the same. If you find this hard to believe, try covering up the rest of the image and looking only at the sharks.

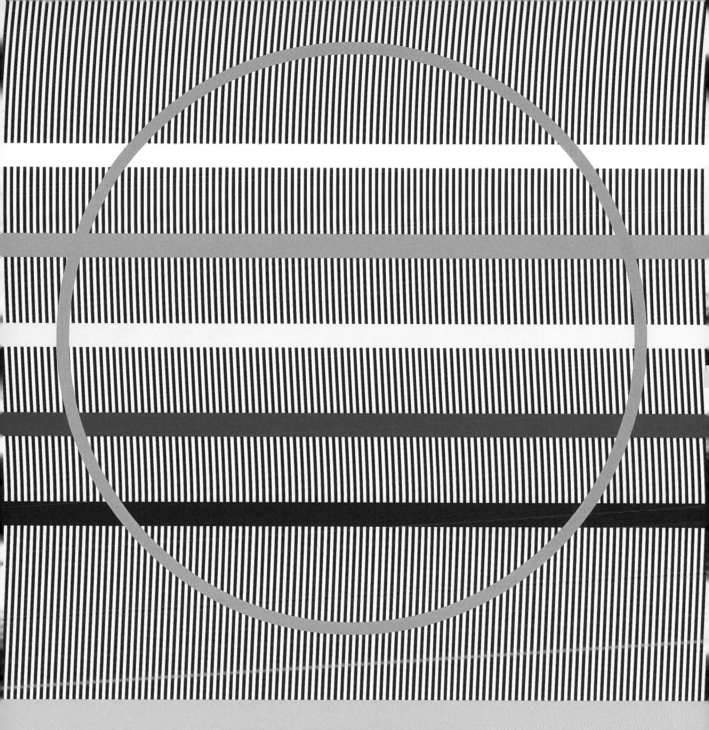

78 Flashing stripes

Look at the big stripes across this image. Can you see little flashes
of white flickering across them? The pattern of tiny black and
white stripes in the background creates this unsettling effect.
You can see another version of the same effect in illusion 32.

79 Impossible cube

Would it be possible to build a cube like this? When you first
look at it, you might think so, but in fact this shape is totally
impossible – it could never exist in three dimensions. The more
you look at it, the clearer this will be.

80 Funny fruit

Can you find five faces hiding in these pieces of fruit? This is
an example of an illusion that plays with your perception of
foreground and background: at first the white spaces are just
holes, but then they turn into the focus of the image.

81 The distance between the stars

The distance between points A and B looks much greater than
the distance between points C and D. But if you measure both,
you'll find that they're exactly the same. Even when you know
this, it's very hard to see it.

82 Raised circle

Both of these images are just made out of circles, but look how different they are – the top one looks completely flat, while the bottom one creates a strong illusion that it's rising up out of the page. If you stare at the bottom one for a while, you can also make it look like a tunnel going down into the page.

83 Surprising smile

There seem to be two smiling faces here, with the bottom one being upside down. But if you turn the book over you'll find that the bottom face is actually frowning. When you look at it upside down your brain "corrects" the image to make it like the top one.

84 How many blocks?

Are there five blocks here, or seven? If you look down the right-hand side you'll get one answer, and if you look down the left you'll get the other! As you follow the lines you'll feel your mind getting confused as what seems to be one block turns into the side of another.

85 Straight lines?

Are the squares tilting in different directions? It seems they are, but in fact they're all completely straight and parallel. If you removed the little diagonal lines the illusion would vanish completely. See illusion 39 for another version of this effect.

86 How many circles?

How many circles can you count in this image? The correct answer is... none at all! There's not a single curved line here, because the image is actually made out of overlapping squares. All you have to do is rotate the square shape lots of times to create the illusion of a circle.

87 Two greens?

Look at the dark green in the top and bottom squares. Now look at
the pale green in the middle ones. They seem to be quite different...
but there's only one shade of green in this picture. The black stripes
and white stripes blend into the green to create the illusion.

88 Ghostly butterfly

Stare at the dot in the middle of the white butterfly for at least 30 seconds, trying not to blink. Then stare at the dot in the middle of the other circle and blink a couple of times. You should see a "shadow" of the butterfly you've been looking at appear inside the circle.

89 Impossible square

Can you see what's weird about this shape? Each side looks normal on
its own, but it would be completely impossible to fit them together like
this. If you start at one corner and follow it around, you'll see why.

90 Leaning clock

Is the clock on the right leaning more than the one on the left? It seems
to be, but it's not: both clocks are standing at exactly the same angle. This
strange illusion is quite subtle but quite powerful too – even when you know
the truth it's hard not to see that slight extra lean on the right-hand clock.

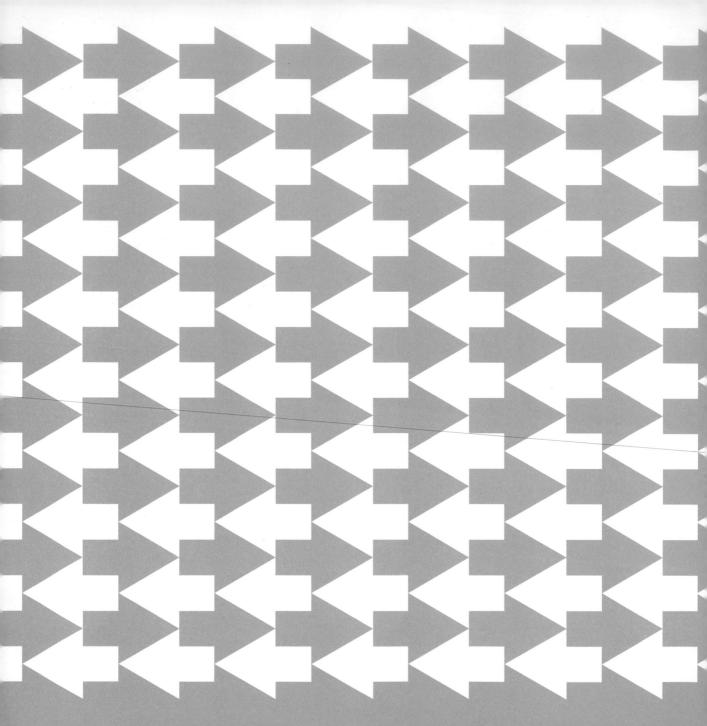

91 Left or right?

Does this image show blue arrows on a white background – or the opposite? The answer, of course, is both. As you look, the image will flip from one to the other, so that the white becomes either the foreground or the background. You'll find it impossible to settle on one or the other.

92 Falling leaves

Look at leaf A, and then at leaf B. The top one seems darker, doesn't it? But both leaves are exactly the same green. This clever illusion works in two ways – the background gradually changes, and so does the shade of the other leaves.

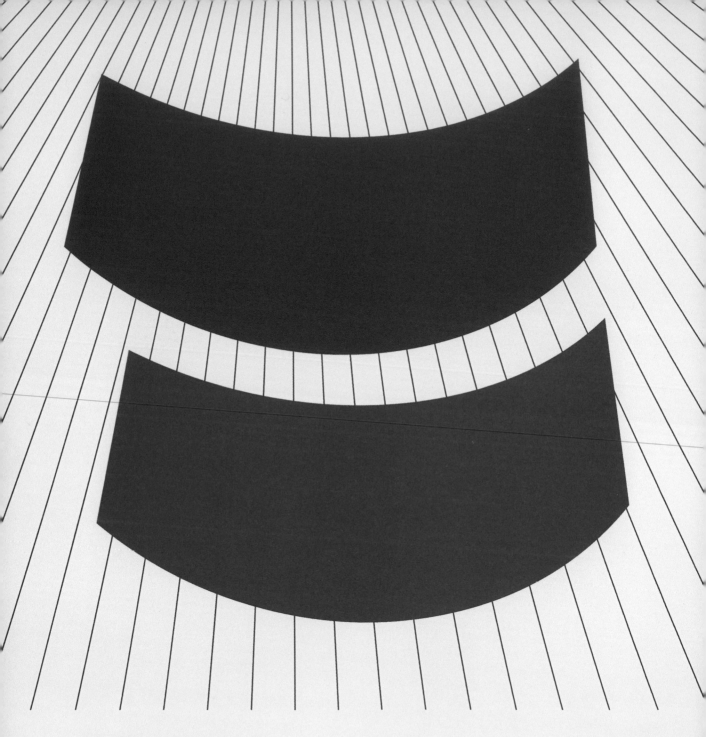

93 Surprising sizes

Is the top shape bigger than the bottom one? At first glance it seems
that it definitely is... but actually both shapes are identical. This is a very
simple but very effective illusion that you can recreate yourself by cutting
out two identical shapes like this and putting one above the other.

94 What's in front?

Which of these shapes is at the front? The fun of this impossible
arrangement is that all of them are, and none of them is. Every time you
look at one that seems to be in front of the others, you'll notice that part
of it is behind them as well. The more you look, the weirder it becomes.

95 Cats' eyes

These three sets of eyes all seem to be looking in different directions. But all three are exactly the same. All you have to do to trick your brain is change the angle of the nose. Try drawing your own version of this illusion – you'll be surprised how easy it is to fool yourself.

96 Ice-cream challenge

Which is further – the distance from A to B or the distance
from C to D? It seems obvious that A to B is further, but both
are exactly the same. You can prove this by measuring.

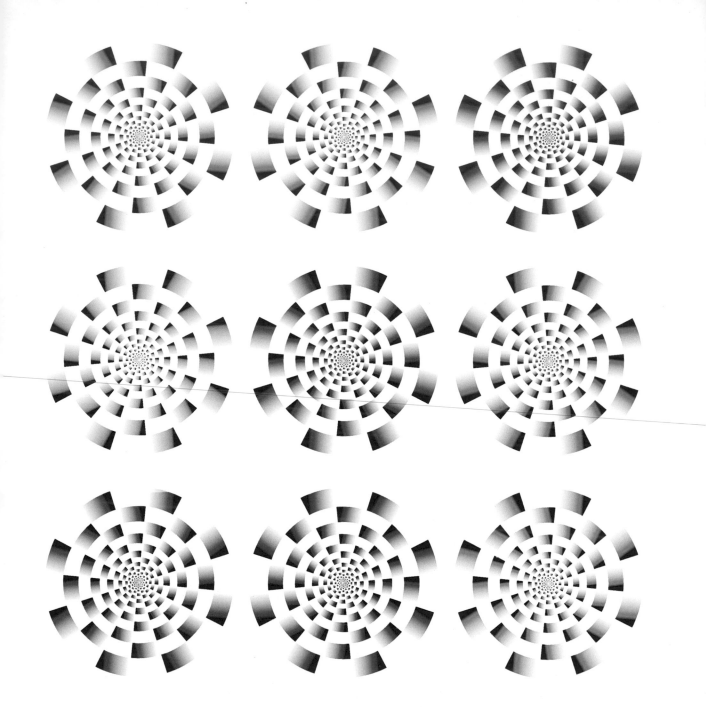

97 Turning circles

Move your eyes around these pages and the circles will seem to rotate.
The one you're looking at will stay still, but you'll see them spinning
out of the corner of your eye. This illusion works a little like illusion 1,
even though the design of the circles is completely different.

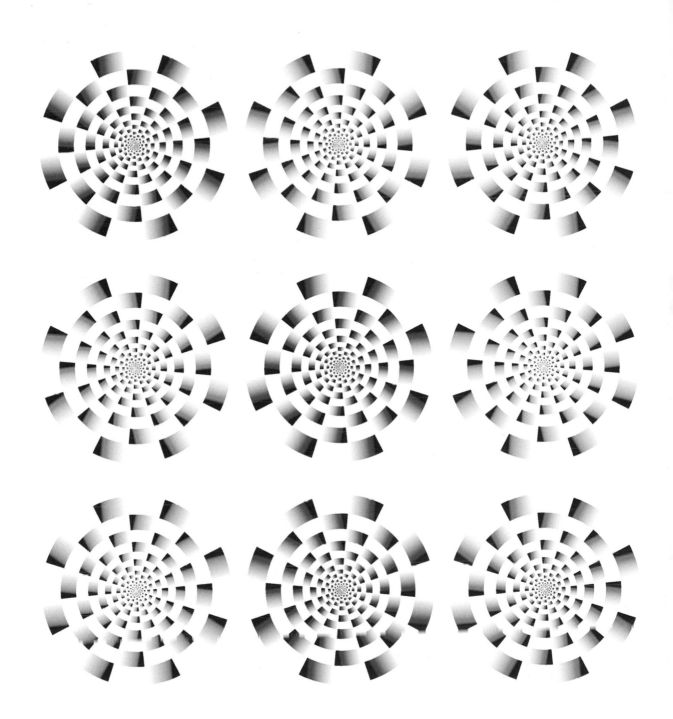

98 Broken circle

Look at the black lines. If you continued them, would they join up to form a circle? It doesn't look as though they would – but in fact you're looking at a perfect circle with a section removed.

99 Upstairs downstairs

What does this image show? A flight of stairs going up, or a flight of
stairs going down? It's actually possible to see it both ways – if you
imagine you're standing at the top looking at a door at the bottom, that's
what you'll see. But you can also make yourself see exactly the opposite!

100 Black and white?

Chess pieces are either black or white, and here you can see one of each. Or so it seems – but actually both pieces on this page are exactly the same shade. This extraordinary effect is created by the changing background. If you can't believe it, cover up everything except the pieces.

101 Chessboard challenge

This is another version of the illusion on the opposite page – and it's just as amazing. The two squares marked with a red dot are exactly the same shade. What we see is one "light" square with a shadow on it, and one "dark" square in a bright light. But they're identical.

A last word about illusions...

When you look at the images in this book,
bear in mind that everyone sees things slightly
differently – an illusion might be very powerful
for one person but less convincing for someone
else. So don't worry if not every image in the
book works for you – the next one probably will.

If you're struggling to make an illusion work,
try looking at it under a brighter light, or
from slightly further away, or out of the corner
of your eye. It's surprising how changing the
way you look at an image can make it much
more effective.

Illusions reveal a lot about the way we see the
world around us. We tend to think that we can
trust our eyes to show us exactly what's there
– but you've now seen 101 reasons why that
simply isn't true.

First published in 2016 by Usborne Publishing Ltd., Usborne House, 83–85 Saffron Hill, London EC1N 8RT,
England. Copyright ©2016 Usborne Publishing Ltd. The name Usborne and the devices ⚑ ⊕ are Trade Marks of
Usborne Publishing Ltd.